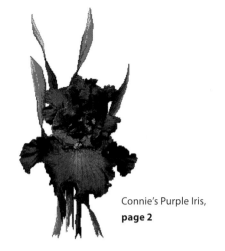

Connie's Purple Iris,
page 2

Introduction

We're sure you will enjoy stitching Marc's four enchanting floral designs featured in this book. Your stitched pieces are sure to become some of your favorite heirlooms, heirlooms you'll be proud to pass down to future generations. Framed and displayed in a grouping, these flower designs form an ever-blooming garden of stately specimens.

Our front cover model, "Connie's Purple Iris," was stitched on Queen Anne's Lace 28-count Jobelan by Wichelt. Marc also suggests stitching over two threads on Queen Anne's Lace 32-count Jobelan by Wichelt. Remember, your finished needlework will be much brighter and better than any picture can be!

Orange Oriental
Poppy, **page 14**

Meet the Designer

Born and raised in the small Norwegian coastal town of Holmestrand, Marc Saastad began his interest of art at a very young age. He developed a love of drawing by age 7, and by 13, he began painting with oils. At age 14, he created his first original cross-stitch design, a field of wildflowers stitched on Aida cloth.

Marc continued his interest in painting while pursuing other career paths. Soon after attending college in Norway, Marc became a member of the Norwegian Merchant Marine for three years, which allowed him to travel the world. After leaving the merchant marines, Marc married and settled down in California, where he found the western coastal areas to be the inspiration for many of his paintings. For 25 years, Marc turned sketches into beautiful paintings and became a very sought-after artist, painting under his middle name Inge.

In 1996, Marc started designing cross-stitch. He was fascinated with the availability of so many brilliant colors in one medium. Many of his designs are creations that have been inspired by his beautiful flower gardens at his home and his many travels throughout the world. His love for flowers is shown in his designs, which are filled with meticulous detail. Marc is famous for using a wide variety of colors, and using DMC and Anchor floss in the same design.

Enchanted Rose,
page 22

Red Tulips, **page 34**

Connie's Purple Iris

Stitch Count
154w x 290h

Approximate Design Size
14-count 11" x 20¾"
16-count 9⅝" x 18⅛"
18-count 8½" x 16"
25-count 6⅛" x 11⅝"
28-count 5½" x 10⅜"
32-count over two threads 9⅝" x 18⅛"

Project Notes
Middle of the design is marked with a white circle at the top of Chart H.
Backstitch direction inside as well as Page Layout.
The pages have no overlap, just line them all up together like the page layout.

Connie's Purple Iris was stitched on Queen Anne's Lace 28-count Jobelan from Wichelt using Anchor and DMC floss. Finished piece was custom framed.

Connie's Purple Iris Color Key

Symbol	Color	Symbol	Color
•	Anchor: 96	◣	DMC: 319
—	Anchor: 97	▢	DMC: 320
♥	Anchor: 98	☺	DMC: 367
▽	Anchor: 99	∣	DMC: 368
.•	Anchor: 100	Z	DMC: 725
⊥	Anchor: 101	☆	Anchor: 872
★	Anchor: 102	▨	Anchor: 876
T	Anchor: 127	◉	DMC: 939
■	Anchor: 152	⁞⁞	DMC: 3032
⊘	Anchor: 178	♡	DMC: 3363

Backstitch

- - - - - - - - - - DMC: 319

————————— DMC: 939

House of White Birches, Berne, Indiana 46711   AnniesAttic.com

House of White Birches, Berne, Indiana 46711   AnniesAttic.com

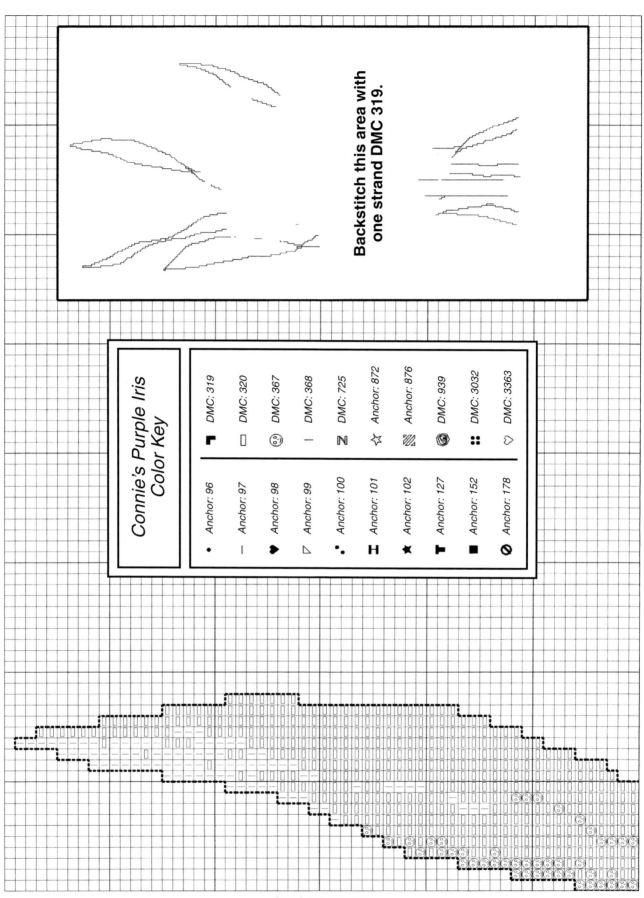

Backstitch this area with one strand DMC 319.

Connie's Purple Iris Color Key

	Anchor		DMC
●	Anchor: 96	◣	DMC: 319
—	Anchor: 97	▯	DMC: 320
❤	Anchor: 98	◉	DMC: 367
◺	Anchor: 99	—	DMC: 368
∴	Anchor: 100	ℕ	DMC: 725
H	Anchor: 101	☆	Anchor: 872
✖	Anchor: 102	▨	Anchor: 876
⊤	Anchor: 127	◉	DMC: 939
■	Anchor: 152	⦂	DMC: 3032
⦸	Anchor: 178	◇	DMC: 3363

Connie's Purple Iris
Chart A

House of White Birches, Berne, Indiana 46711   AnniesAttic.com

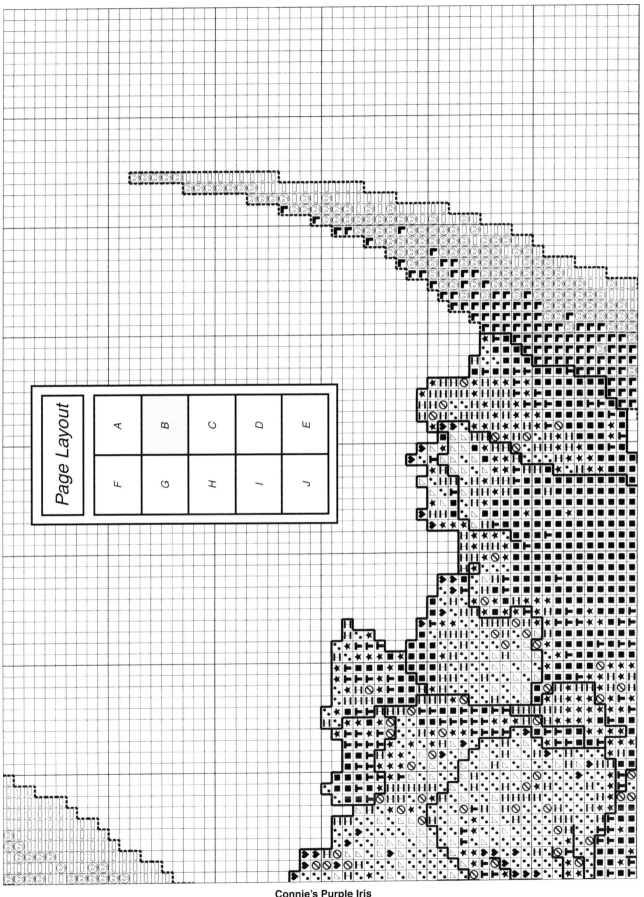

Page Layout

| A | B | C | D | E |
| F | G | H | I | J |

Connie's Purple Iris
Chart B

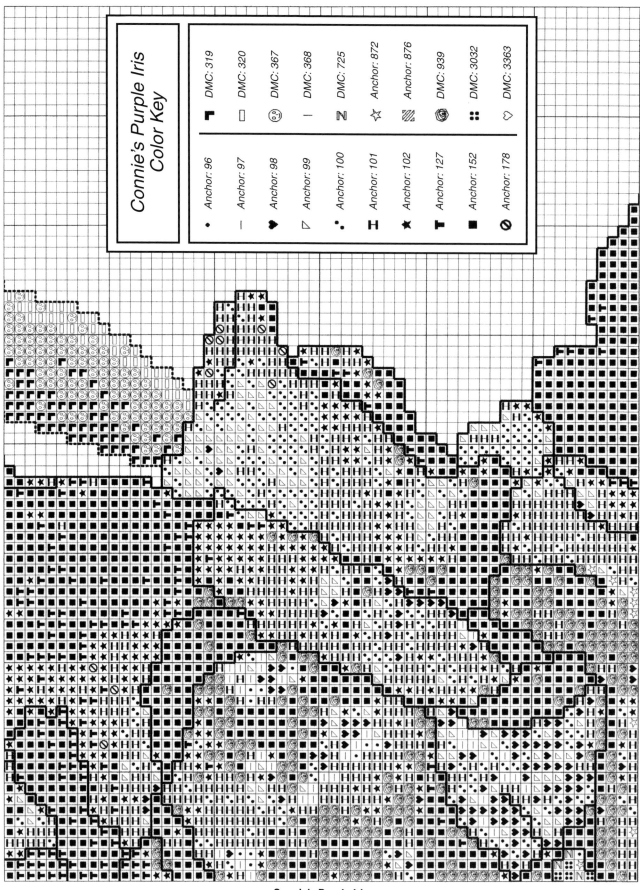

Connie's Purple Iris Color Key

	Anchor: 96		DMC: 319
	Anchor: 97		DMC: 320
	Anchor: 98		DMC: 367
	Anchor: 99		DMC: 368
	Anchor: 100		DMC: 725
	Anchor: 101		Anchor: 872
	Anchor: 102		Anchor: 876
	Anchor: 127		DMC: 939
	Anchor: 152		DMC: 3032
	Anchor: 178		DMC: 3363

Connie's Purple Iris
Chart C

House of White Birches, Berne, Indiana 46711   AnniesAttic.com

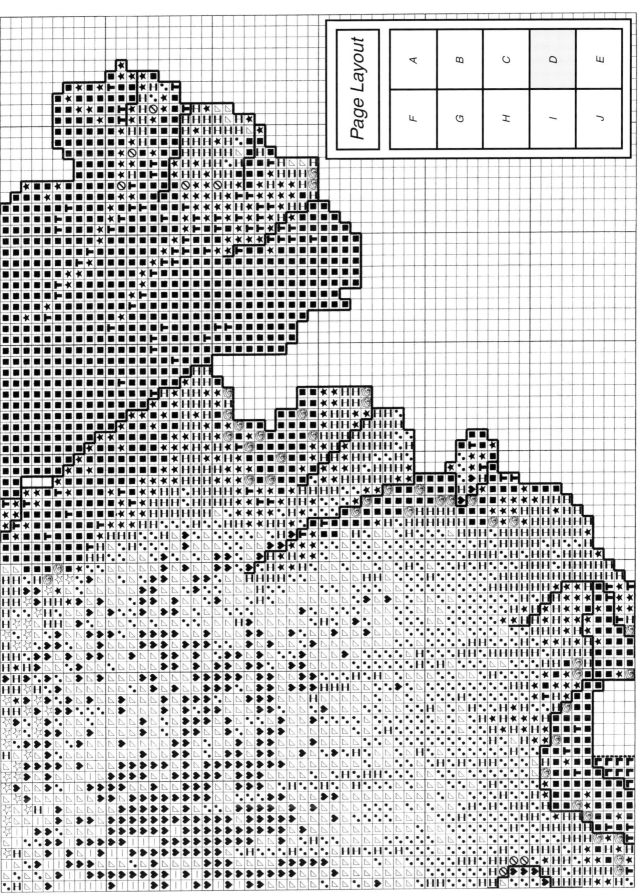

Connie's Purple Iris
Chart D

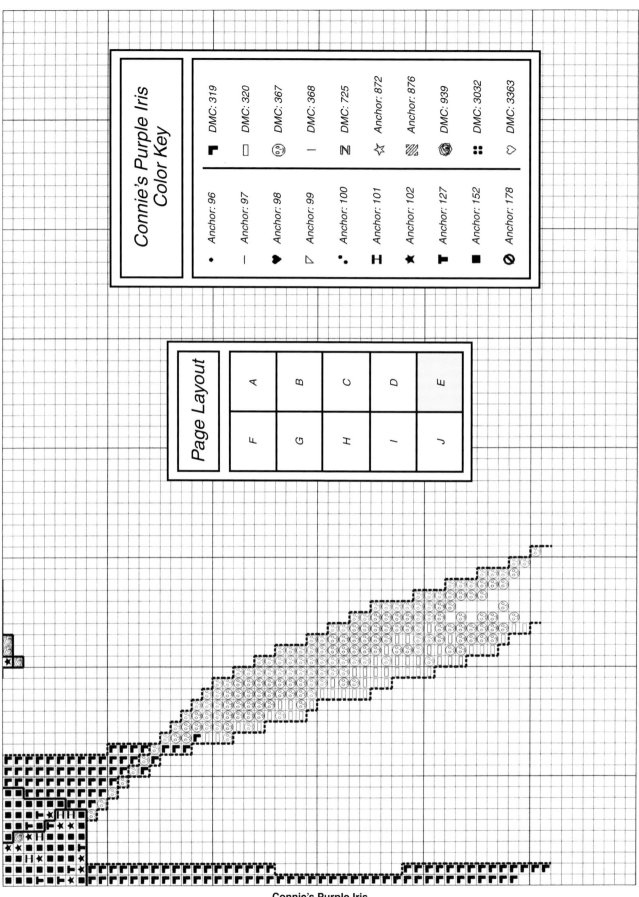

Connie's Purple Iris
Chart E

House of White Birches, Berne, Indiana 46711   AnniesAttic.com

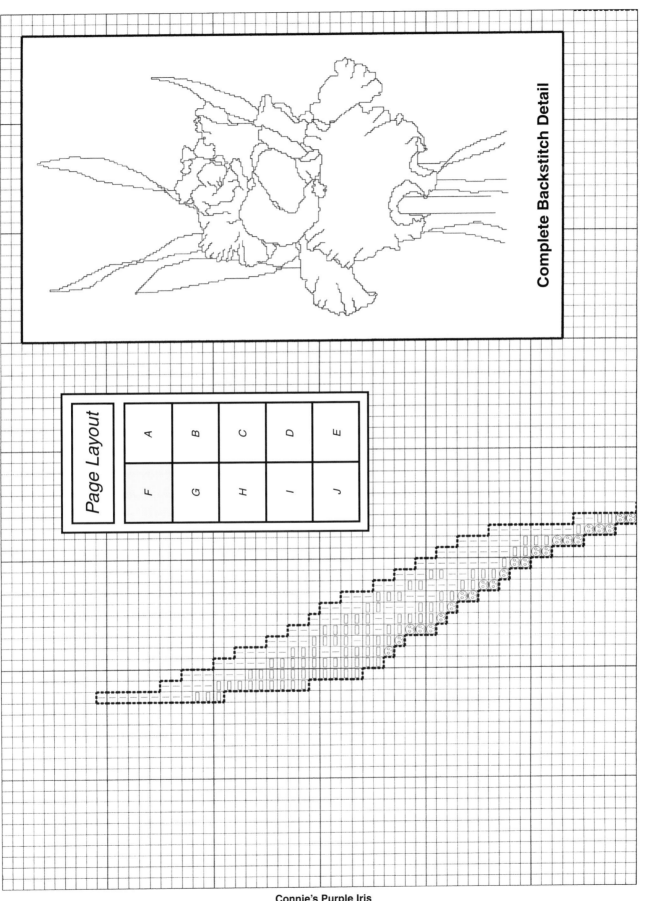

Complete Backstitch Detail

Page Layout				
A	B	C	D	E
F	G	H	I	J

Connie's Purple Iris
Chart F

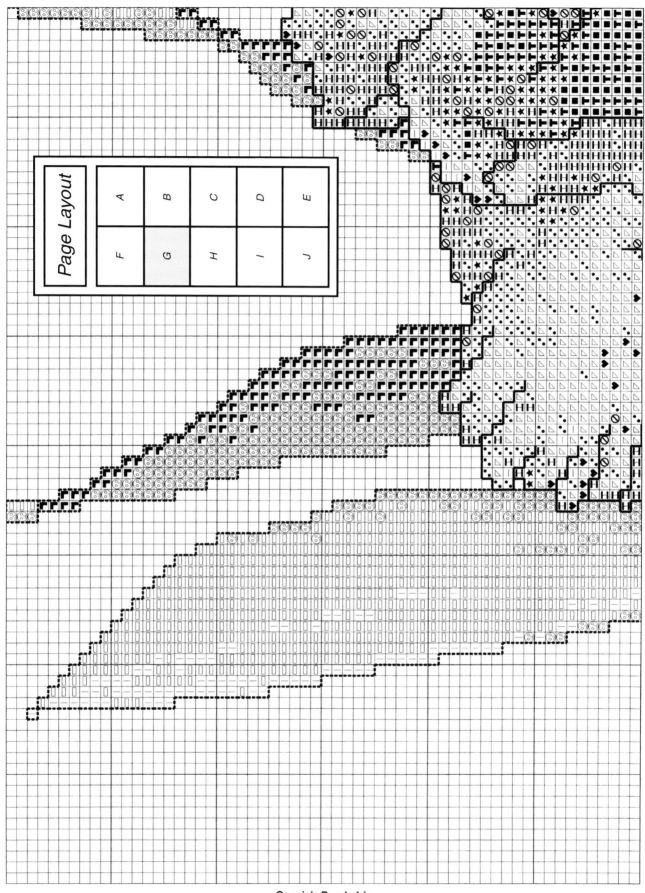

A	B	C	D	E
F	G	H	I	J

Page Layout

Connie's Purple Iris
Chart G

House of White Birches, Berne, Indiana 46711 AnniesAttic.com

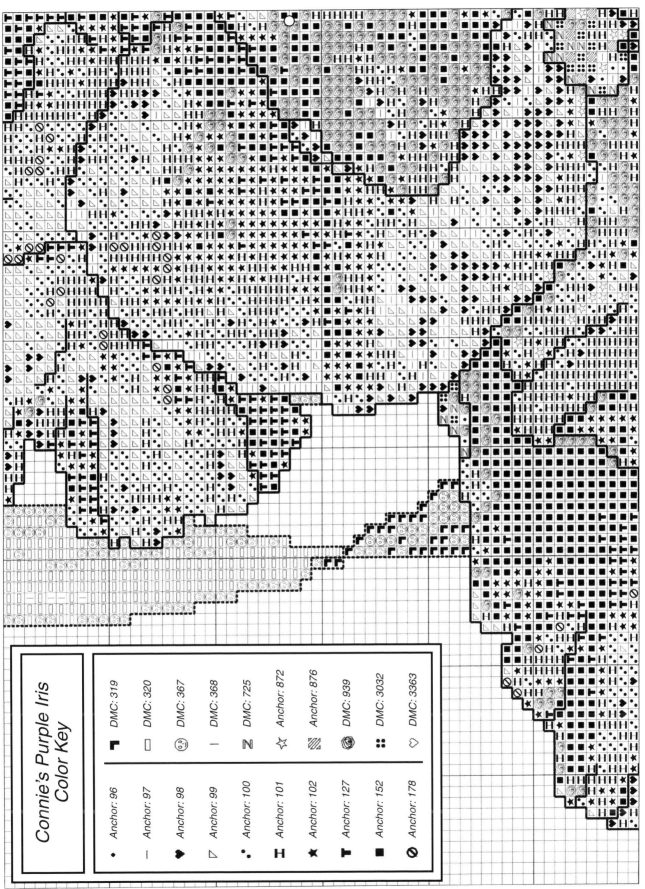

Connie's Purple Iris Color Key

⌐	DMC: 319	•	Anchor: 96
☐	DMC: 320	I	Anchor: 97
☺	DMC: 367	◆	Anchor: 98
—	DMC: 368	△	Anchor: 99
N	DMC: 725	•.	Anchor: 100
☆	Anchor: 872	H	Anchor: 101
▨	Anchor: 876	★	Anchor: 102
◉	DMC: 939	⌐	Anchor: 127
∷	DMC: 3032	■	Anchor: 152
◇	DMC: 3363	⊘	Anchor: 178

Connie's Purple Iris
Chart H

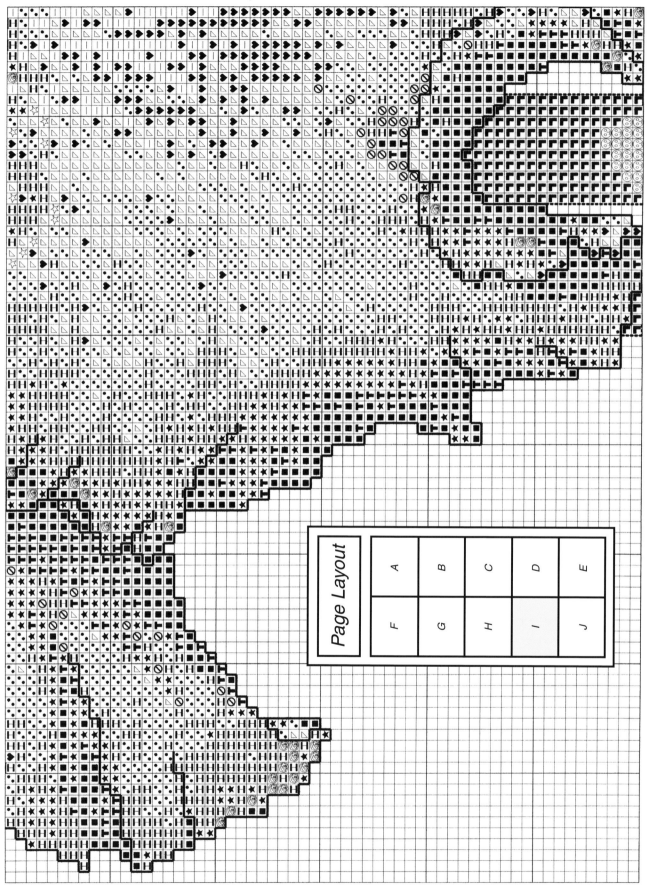

Page Layout

A	B	C	D	E
F	G	H	I	J

Connie's Purple Iris
Chart I

House of White Birches, Berne, Indiana 46711   AnniesAttic.com

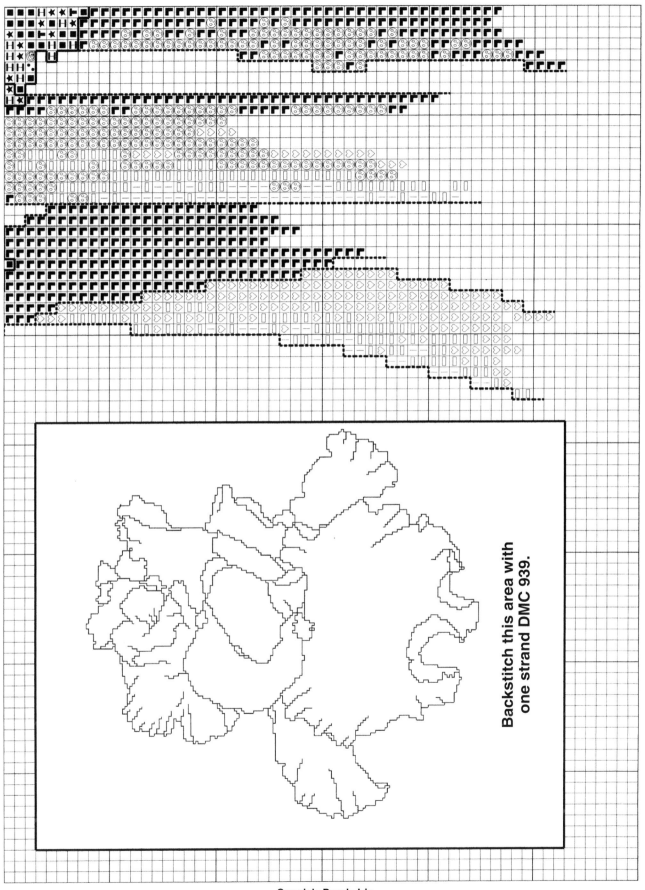

Backstitch this area with one strand DMC 939.

Connie's Purple Iris
Chart J

Orange Oriental Poppy

Stitch Count
158w x 158h

Approximate Design Size
14-count 11¼" x 11¼"
16-count 9⅞" x 9⅞"
18-count 8¾" x 8¾"
25-count 6⅜" x 6⅜"
28-count 5⅝" x 5⅝"
32-count over two threads 9⅞" x 9⅞"

Project Notes
Middle of the design is marked with a white half circle on the bottom of Chart B and
   a half circle at the top of Chart E.
Backstitch direction inside as well as Page Layout.
The pages have no overlap, just line them all up together like the page layout.

Orange Oriental Poppy Color Key

♡	Anchor: 46	▽	DMC: 522	▲	Anchor: 897	◨	DMC: 987
✚	Anchor: 47	⊘	DMC: 561	◎	DMC: 898	◤	DMC: 988
♥	Anchor: 102	T	DMC: 580	☆	DMC: 900	◖	Anchor: 1015
■	DMC: 310	✕	DMC: 606	⊞	DMC: 906	←	DMC: 3041
⠒	Anchor: 316	▭	DMC: 608	●	DMC: 924	✪	DMC: 3051
⊖	DMC: 320	◉	DMC: 645	▨	DMC: 934	∪	DMC: 3340
\	Anchor: 333	ⵂ	DMC: 646	ℤ	DMC: 936	⁄	DMC: 3347
◑	Anchor: 334	ⵗ	DMC: 702	⌂	DMC: 937	+	DMC: 3348
⁑	Anchor: 335	∿	DMC: 720	↔	DMC: 939	◕	DMC: 3362
⬈	DMC: 367	★	DMC: 740	⧓	DMC: 946	⠶	DMC: 3363
⌐	DMC: 371	◣	DMC: 741	⧚	DMC: 947	|	DMC: 3364
⊏	DMC: 470	⋈	DMC: 742	⊂	DMC: 970	◢	DMC: 3799
=	DMC: 471	◥	DMC: 823	▽	DMC: 971	⧄	DMC: 3818
⊞	DMC: 501	∴	DMC: 844	◀	DMC: 972	⊞	Anchor: 9046

Backstitch

————————	DMC: 902
- - - - - - - -	DMC: 936

House of White Birches, Berne, Indiana 46711   AnniesAttic.com

House of White Birches, Berne, Indiana 46711 AnniesAttic.com

Backstitch this area with one strand DMC 902.

Page Layout

D	A
E	B
F	C

Complete Backstitch Detail

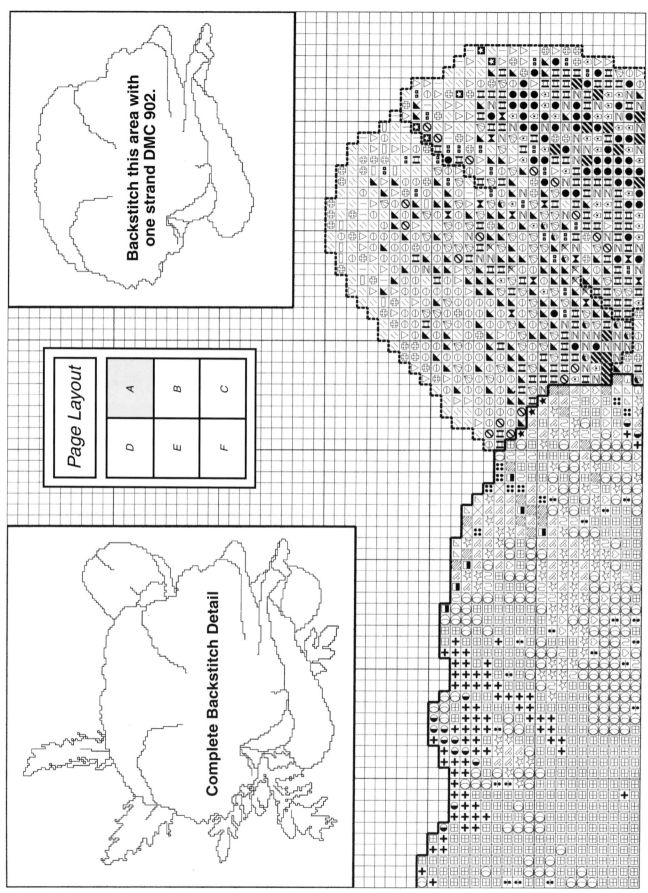

Orange Oriental Poppy
Chart A

House of White Birches, Berne, Indiana 46711   AnniesAttic.com

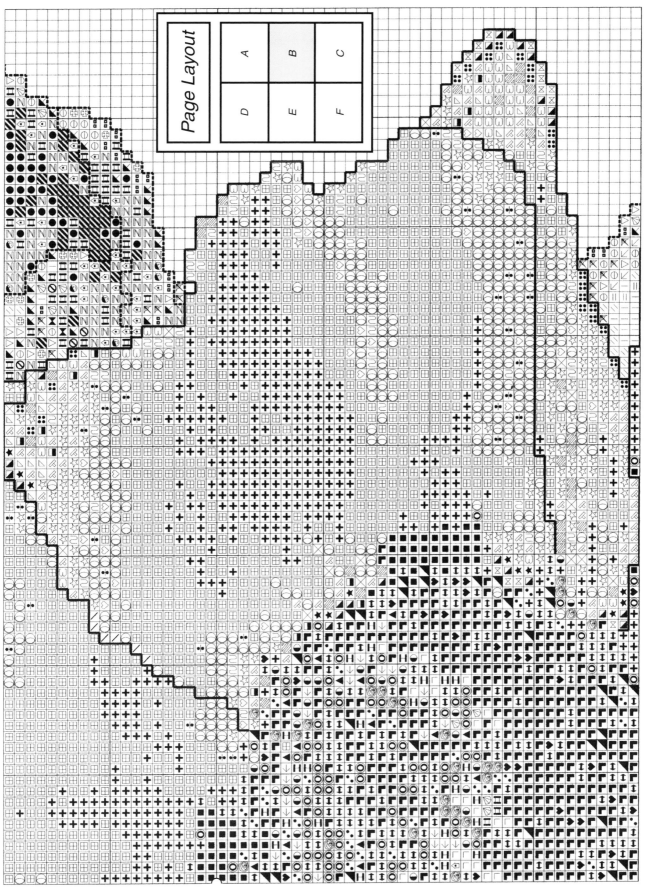

Page Layout

A	B	C
D	E	F

Orange Oriental Poppy
Chart B

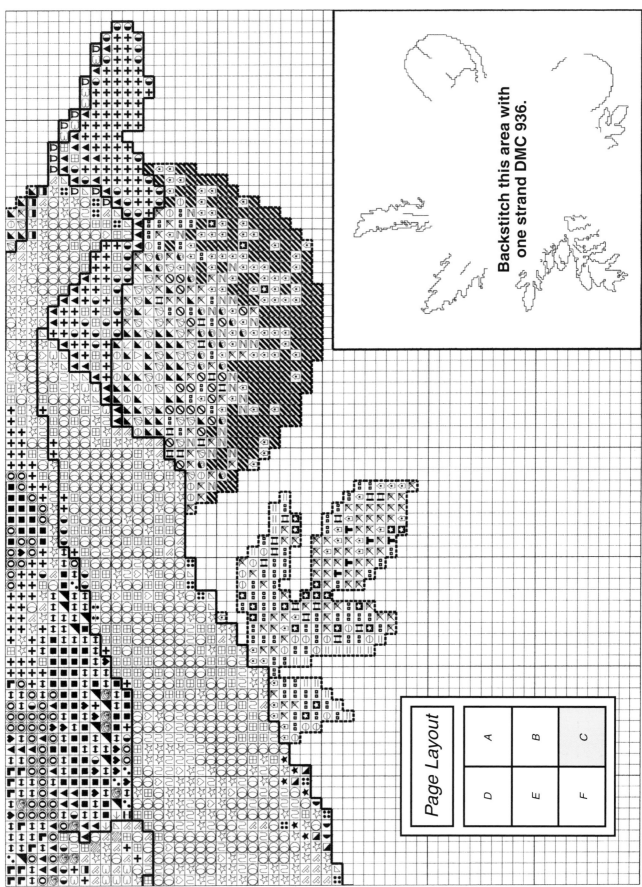

Backstitch this area with one strand DMC 936.

Page Layout

D	A
E	B
F	C

Orange Oriental Poppy
Chart C

House of White Birches, Berne, Indiana 46711   AnniesAttic.com

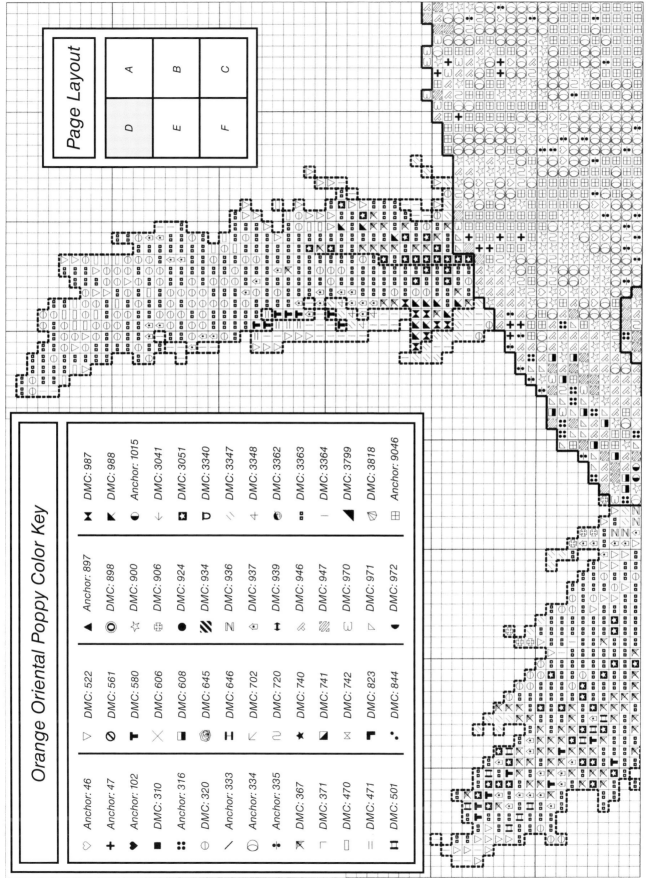

Page Layout

A	B	C
D	E	F

Orange Oriental Poppy Color Key

Symbol	Color	Symbol	Color	Symbol	Color	Symbol	Color
◇	Anchor: 46	▷	DMC: 522	◀	Anchor: 897	✖	DMC: 987
✚	Anchor: 47	⊘	DMC: 561	◎	DMC: 898	◤	DMC: 988
◆	Anchor: 102	⊩	DMC: 580	☆	DMC: 900	◐	Anchor: 1015
■	DMC: 310	✕	DMC: 606	✠	DMC: 906	↓	DMC: 3041
⠿	Anchor: 316	▮	DMC: 608	●	DMC: 924	✪	DMC: 3051
◐	DMC: 320	✿	DMC: 645	◥	DMC: 934	▷	DMC: 3340
/	Anchor: 333	H	DMC: 646	N	DMC: 936	＼	DMC: 3347
⊖	Anchor: 334	↙	DMC: 702	◁	DMC: 937	✛	DMC: 3348
◆	Anchor: 335	⌇	DMC: 720	⇕	DMC: 939	◕	DMC: 3362
✗	DMC: 367	★	DMC: 740	⬩	DMC: 946	◘	DMC: 3363
⌐	DMC: 371	◢	DMC: 741	⟋	DMC: 947	—	DMC: 3364
▯	DMC: 470	⊠	DMC: 742	⫽	DMC: 970	◣	DMC: 3799
＝	DMC: 471	⌐	DMC: 823	⌇	DMC: 971	⬗	DMC: 3818
Ⅱ	DMC: 501	∴	DMC: 844	△	DMC: 972	⊞	Anchor: 9046

Orange Oriental Poppy

Chart D

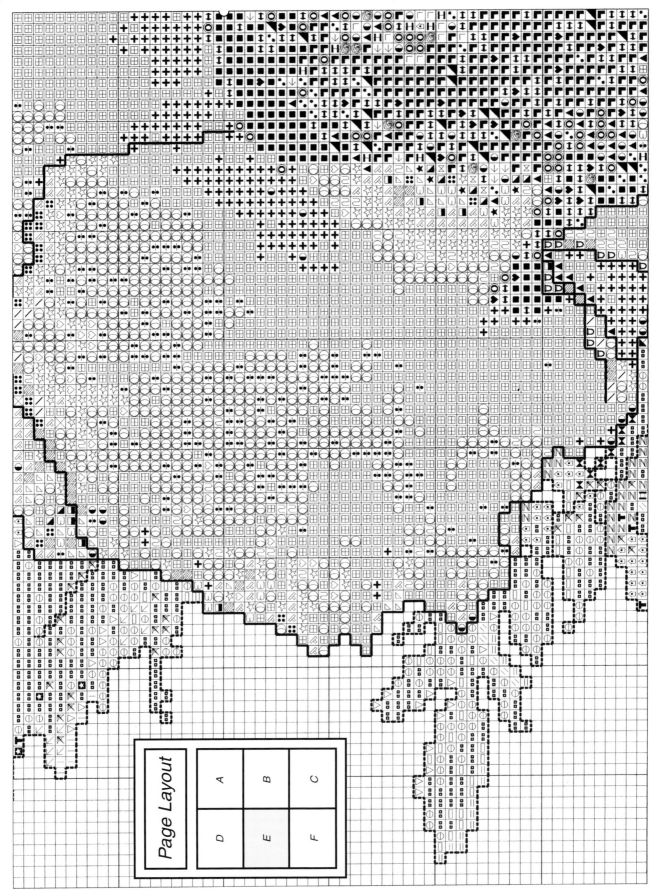

Page Layout

	A	B	C
D	E	F	

Orange Oriental Poppy
Chart E

House of White Birches, Berne, Indiana 46711   AnniesAttic.com

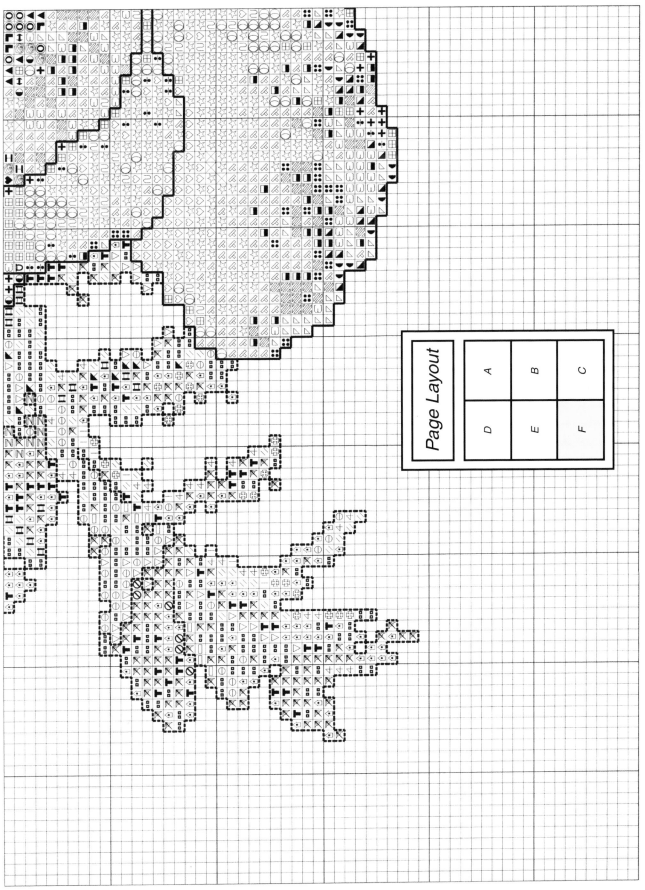

Page Layout

A	B	C
D	E	F

Orange Oriental Poppy
Chart F

Enchanted Rose

Stitch Count
176w x 297h

Approximate Design Size
14-count 12½" x 21¼"
16-count 11" x 18½"
18-count 9¾" x 16½"
25-count 7" x 11⅞"
28-count 6¼" x 10⅝"
32-count over two threads 11" x 18½"

Project Notes
Middle of the design is marked with a white circle at the bottom
of Chart D.
Backstitch direction inside as well as Page Layout.
The pages have no overlap, just line them all up together like
the page layout.

Enchanted Rose Color Key

Symbol	Color	Symbol	Color
◣	Anchor: 264	∷	DMC: 740
♡	Anchor: 265			DMC: 741
◖	Anchor: 266	∩	DMC: 742
Z	Anchor: 267	▬	DMC: 900
◛	Anchor: 268	■	DMC: 902
▨	Anchor: 269	⌂	DMC: 918
▢	Anchor: 304	T	DMC: 919
☆	DMC: 307	♥	DMC: 934
Ⓗ	DMC: 321	★	DMC: 936
●	Anchor: 332	◍	DMC: 937
╲	DMC: 444	▧	DMC: 972
⊘	DMC: 469	•	DMC: 973
✕	DMC: 470	▲	DMC: 3346
☺	DMC: 471	╲	DMC: 3347
▭	DMC: 522	◢	DMC: 3857
◉	DMC: 581		

Backstitch
------------- DMC: 936
——————— DMC: 3857

House of White Birches, Berne, Indiana 46711   AnniesAttic.com

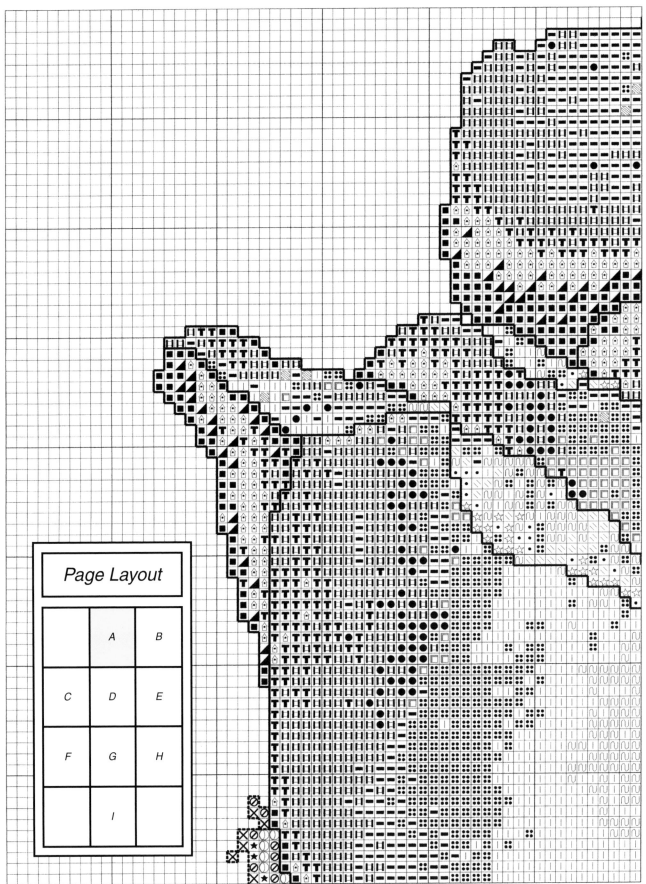

Page Layout

	A	B
C	D	E
F	G	H
	I	

Enchanted Rose
Chart A

House of White Birches, Berne, Indiana 46711   AnniesAttic.com

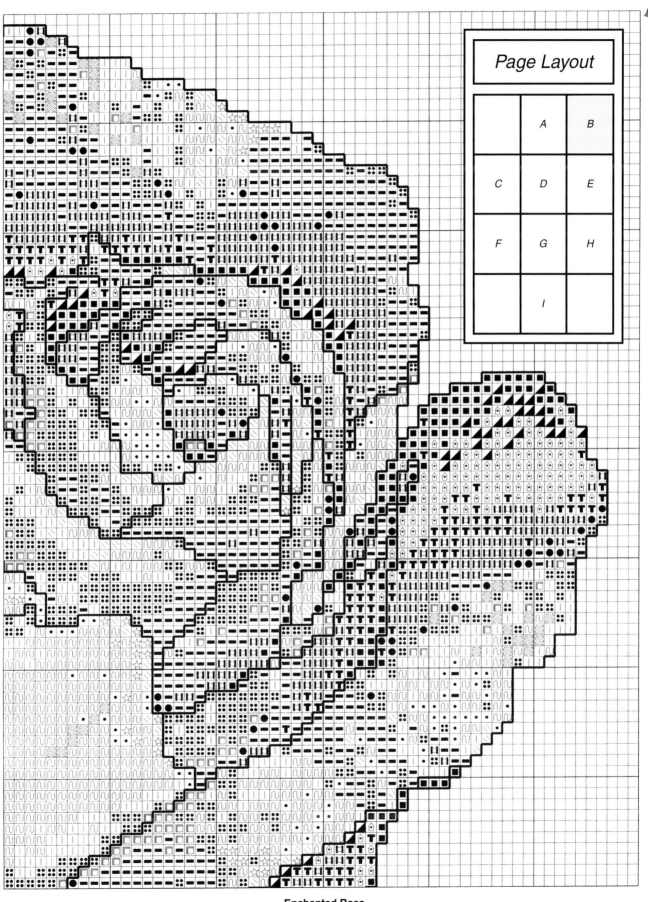

Page Layout

	A	B
C	D	E
F	G	H
	I	

Enchanted Rose
Chart B

Splendid Florals

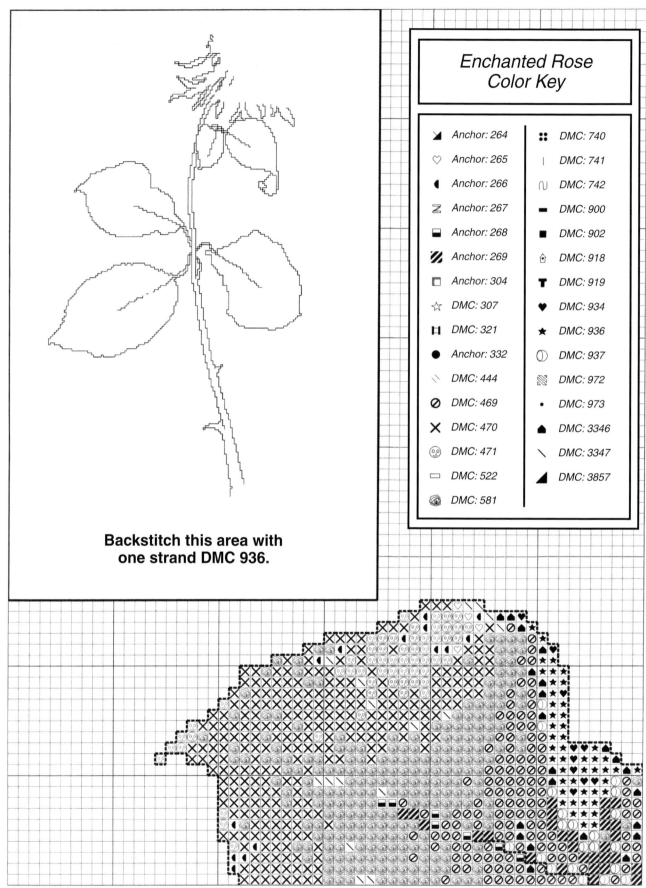

Enchanted Rose
Color Key

◢	Anchor: 264	::	DMC: 740
♡	Anchor: 265	ǀ	DMC: 741
◖	Anchor: 266	∩	DMC: 742
Z	Anchor: 267	▬	DMC: 900
⊟	Anchor: 268	■	DMC: 902
▨	Anchor: 269	⌂	DMC: 918
▢	Anchor: 304	T	DMC: 919
☆	DMC: 307	♥	DMC: 934
H	DMC: 321	★	DMC: 936
●	Anchor: 332	◖	DMC: 937
╲	DMC: 444	▨	DMC: 972
⊘	DMC: 469	•	DMC: 973
✕	DMC: 470	▲	DMC: 3346
☺	DMC: 471	╲	DMC: 3347
⊡	DMC: 522	◣	DMC: 3857
◉	DMC: 581		

**Backstitch this area with
one strand DMC 936.**

Enchanted Rose
Chart C

House of White Birches, Berne, Indiana 46711   AnniesAttic.com

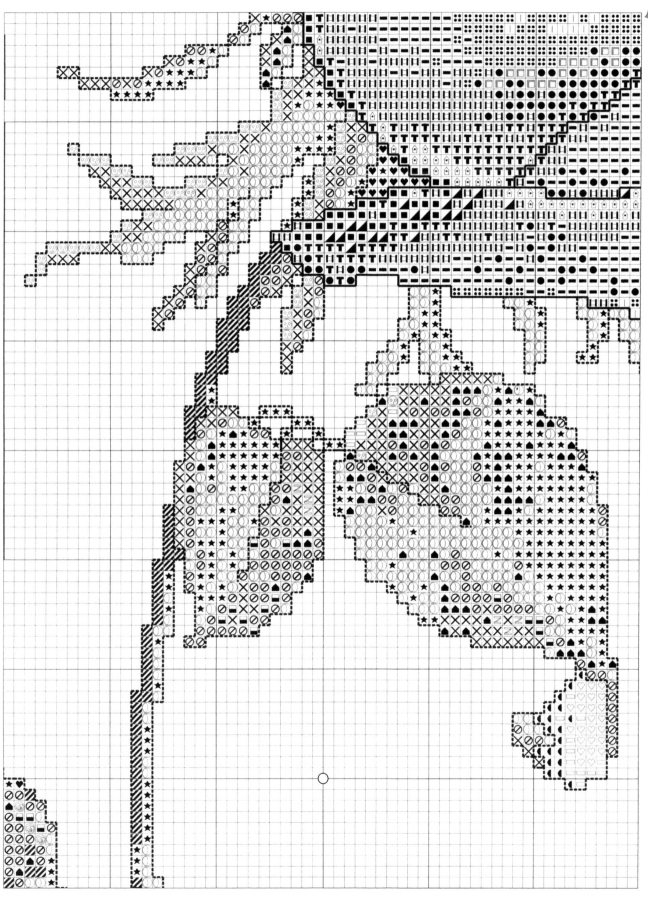

Enchanted Rose
Chart D

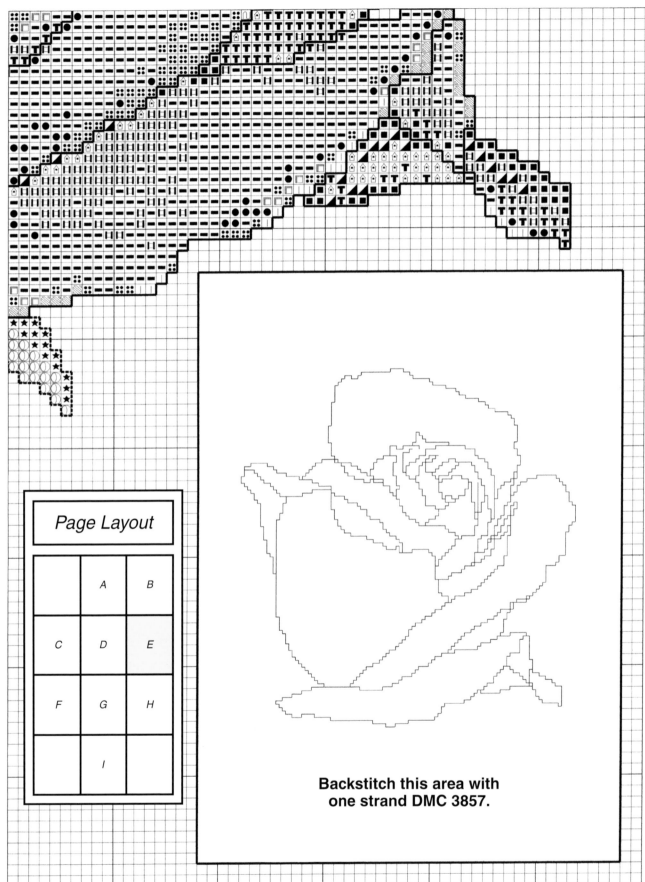

Page Layout

	A	B
C	D	E
F	G	H
	I	

Backstitch this area with one strand DMC 3857.

Enchanted Rose
Chart E

House of White Birches, Berne, Indiana 46711   AnniesAttic.com

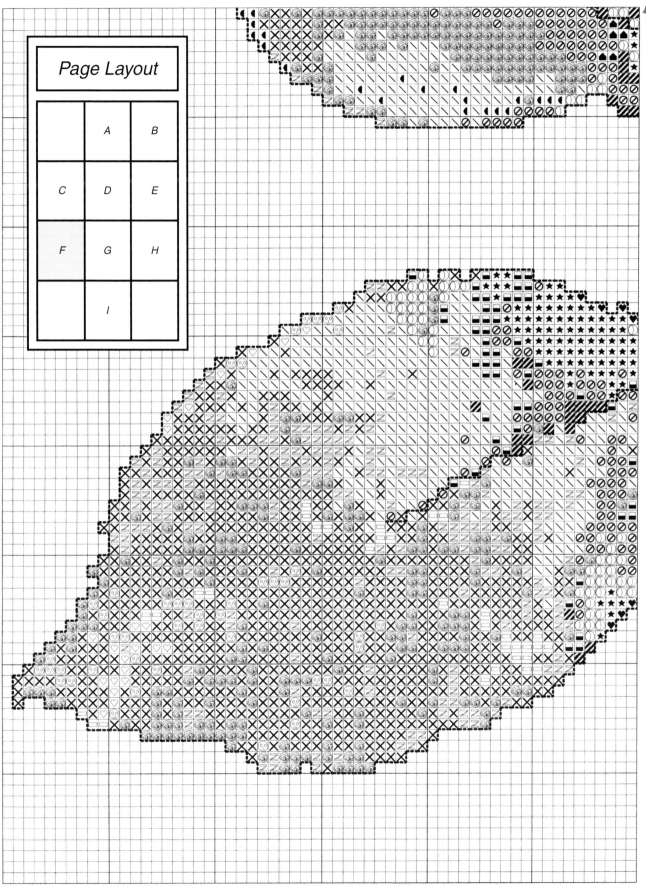

Enchanted Rose
Chart F

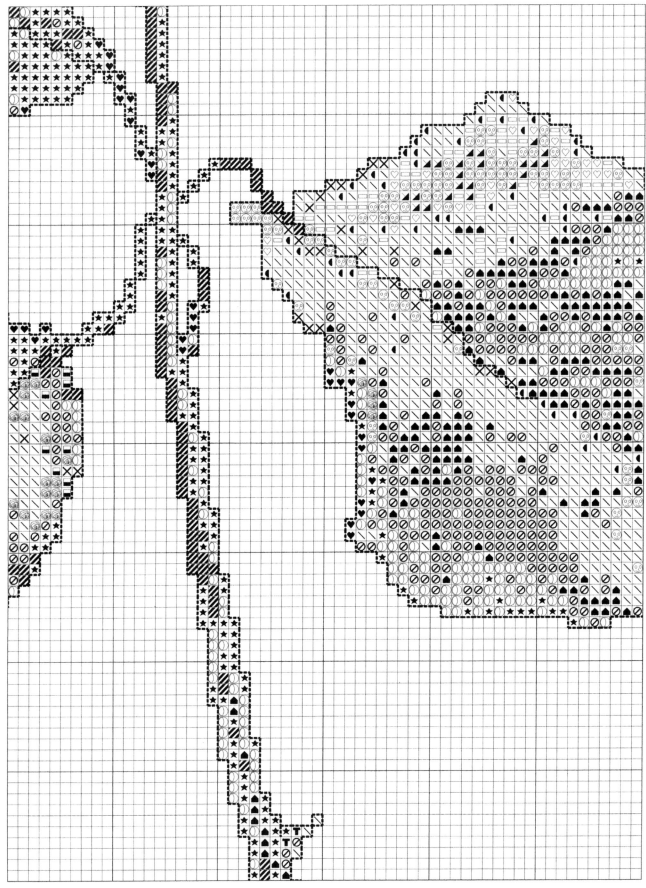

Enchanted Rose
Chart G

House of White Birches, Berne, Indiana 46711   AnniesAttic.com

Complete Backstitch Detail

Enchanted Rose
Chart H

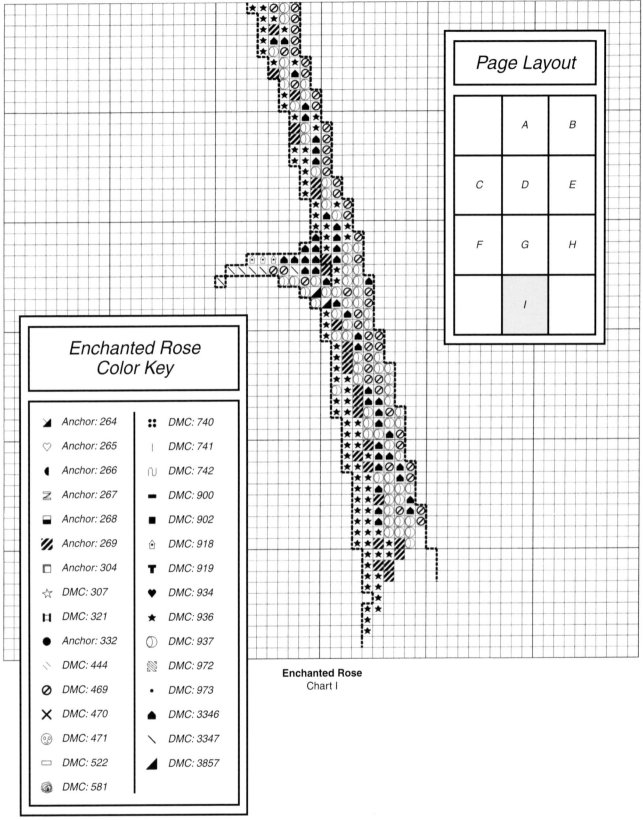

Page Layout

	A	B
C	D	E
F	G	H
	I	

Enchanted Rose
Color Key

◣	Anchor: 264	▪▪	DMC: 740
♡	Anchor: 265	ǀ	DMC: 741
◖	Anchor: 266	∩	DMC: 742
Z	Anchor: 267	▬	DMC: 900
▭	Anchor: 268	■	DMC: 902
▨	Anchor: 269	⌂	DMC: 918
▢	Anchor: 304	T	DMC: 919
☆	DMC: 307	♥	DMC: 934
H	DMC: 321	★	DMC: 936
●	Anchor: 332	◍	DMC: 937
╲	DMC: 444	▨	DMC: 972
⊘	DMC: 469	•	DMC: 973
✕	DMC: 470	▲	DMC: 3346
☺	DMC: 471	╲	DMC: 3347
▭	DMC: 522	◢	DMC: 3857
◉	DMC: 581		

Enchanted Rose
Chart I

House of White Birches, Berne, Indiana 46711   AnniesAttic.com

Red Tulips

Stitch Count
177w x 278h

Approximate Design Size
14-count 12⅝" x 19⅞"
16-count 11" x 17⅜"
18-count 9⅞" x 15½"
25-count 7" x 11⅛"
28-count 6⅜" x 10"
32-count over two threads 11" x 17⅜"

Project Notes
Middle of the design is marked with a white circle on Chart E.
Backstitch direction inside as well as Page Layout.
The pages have no overlap, just line them all up together like the page layout.

Red Tulips Color Key

Z Anchor: 20	Є DMC: 367	DMC: 902
X Anchor: 22	DMC: 368	DMC: 987
⊘ Anchor: 44	▭ DMC: 369	DMC: 988
★ Anchor: 45	♥ DMC: 501	■ DMC: 3345
♡ Anchor: 214	DMC: 502	− DMC: 3348
◑ Anchor: 215	DMC: 503	▽ DMC: 3364
▬ Anchor: 216	• DMC: 522	● DMC: 3371
◤ Anchor: 259	① DMC: 666	☆ DMC: 3801
∩ DMC: 304	♥ DMC: 814	∷ DMC: 3815
= DMC: 320	T DMC: 815	Anchor: 9046
I DMC: 321		

Backstitch

—————— Anchor: 45
- - - - - - DMC: 319

House of White Birches, Berne, Indiana 46711   AnniesAttic.com

House of White Birches, Berne, Indiana 46711   AnniesAttic.com

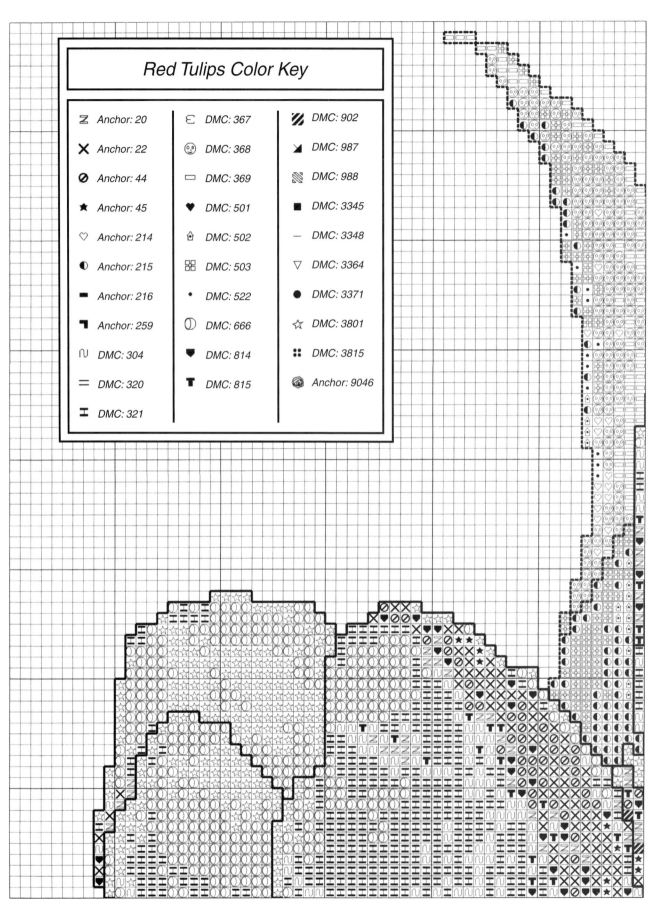

Red Tulips Color Key

Z	Anchor: 20	Ɛ	DMC: 367	▨	DMC: 902
✕	Anchor: 22	☺	DMC: 368	◣	DMC: 987
⊘	Anchor: 44	▭	DMC: 369	▧	DMC: 988
★	Anchor: 45	♥	DMC: 501	■	DMC: 3345
♡	Anchor: 214	⌂	DMC: 502	—	DMC: 3348
◑	Anchor: 215	⊞	DMC: 503	▽	DMC: 3364
▬	Anchor: 216	•	DMC: 522	●	DMC: 3371
◥	Anchor: 259	◍	DMC: 666	☆	DMC: 3801
∩	DMC: 304	♥	DMC: 814	⠿	DMC: 3815
═	DMC: 320	T	DMC: 815	◉	Anchor: 9046
ⱶ	DMC: 321				

Red Tulips
Chart A

House of White Birches, Berne, Indiana 46711   AnniesAttic.com

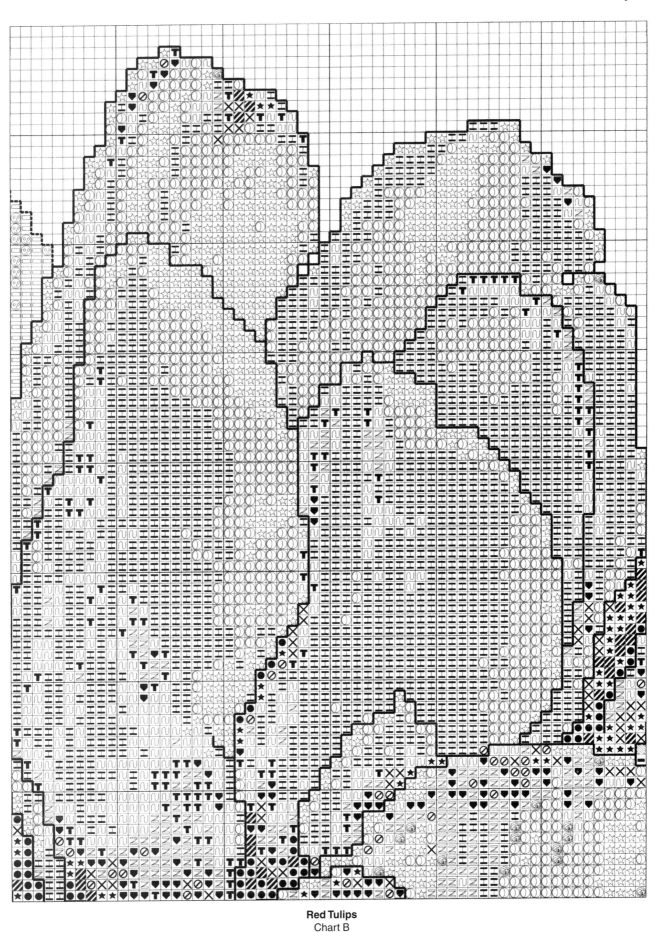

Red Tulips
Chart B

House of White Birches, Berne, Indiana 46711   AnniesAttic.com

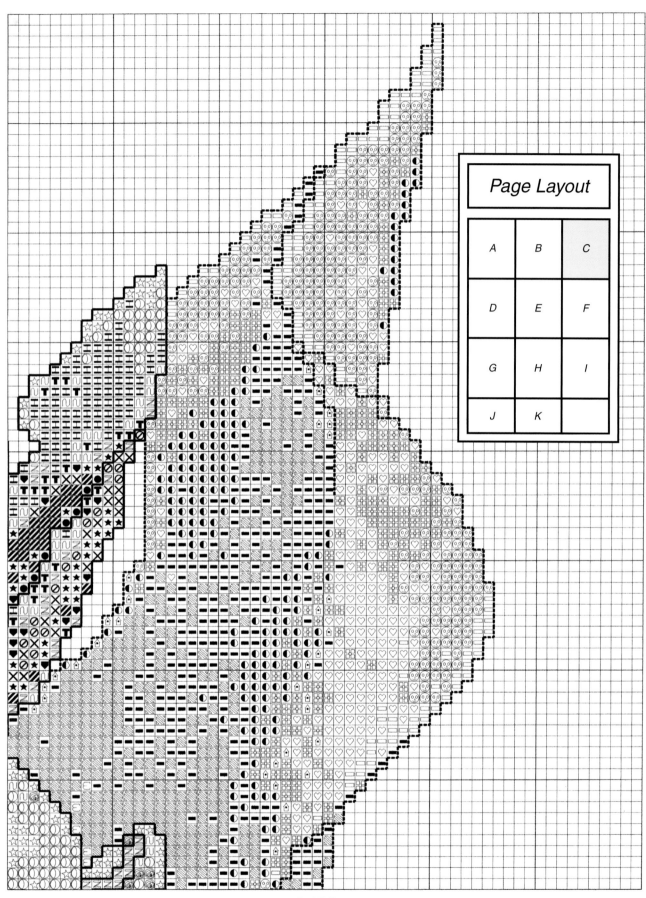

Page Layout

A	B	C
D	E	F
G	H	I
J	K	

Red Tulips
Chart C

House of White Birches, Berne, Indiana 46711   AnniesAttic.com

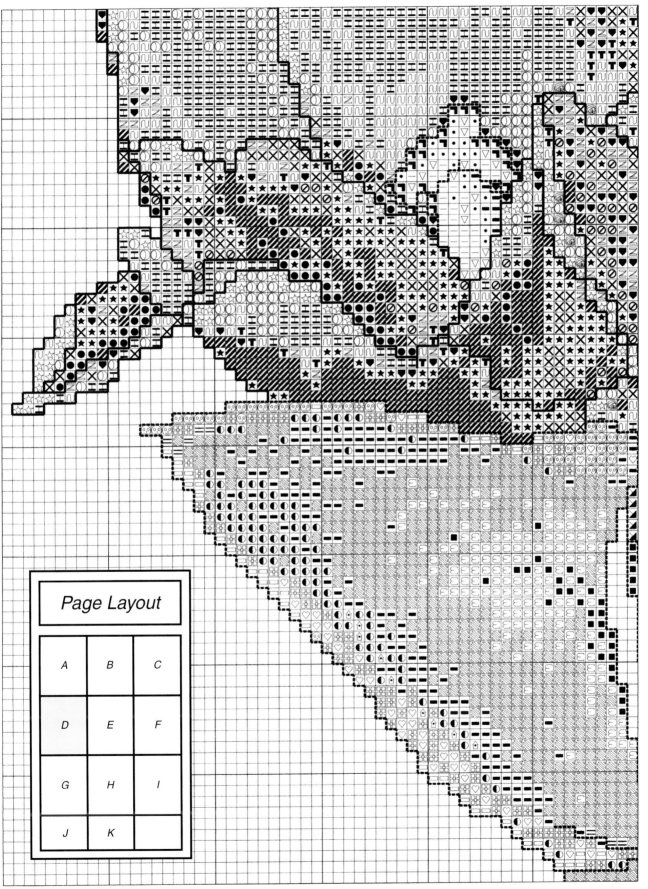

Red Tulips
Chart D

Page Layout

A	B	C
D	E	F
G	H	I
J	K	

House of White Birches, Berne, Indiana 46711   AnniesAttic.com

Red Tulips
Chart E

House of White Birches, Berne, Indiana 46711   AnniesAttic.com

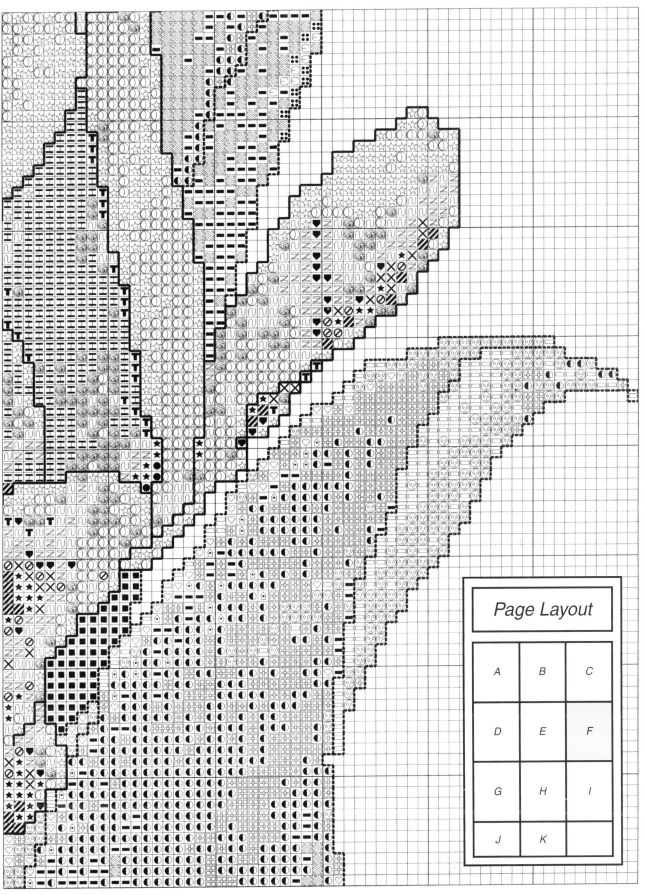

Page Layout

A	B	C
D	E	F
G	H	I
J	K	

Red Tulips
Chart F

House of White Birches, Berne, Indiana 46711   AnniesAttic.com

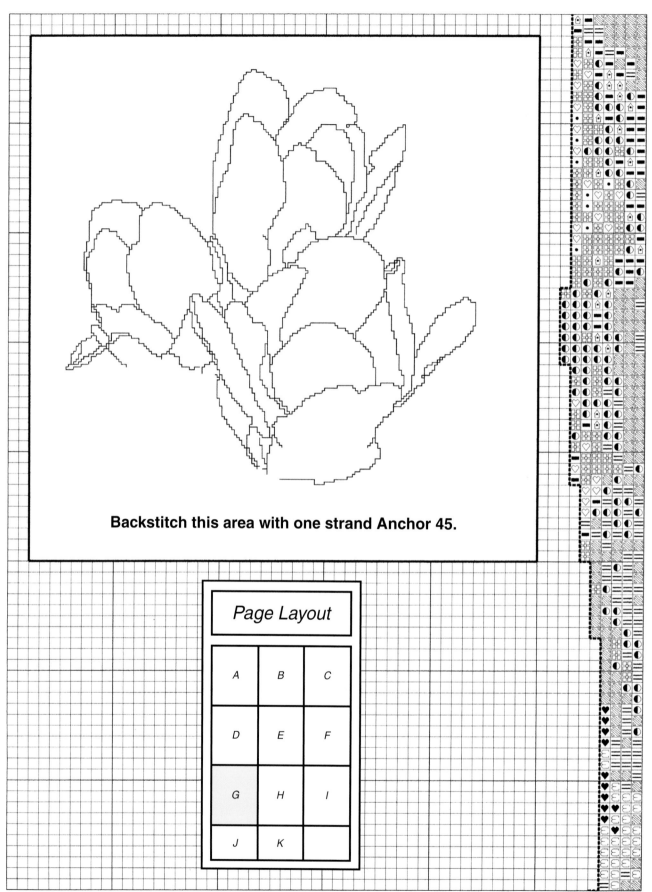

Backstitch this area with one strand Anchor 45.

Page Layout

A	B	C
D	E	F
G	H	I
J	K	

Red Tulips
Chart G

House of White Birches, Berne, Indiana 46711   AnniesAttic.com

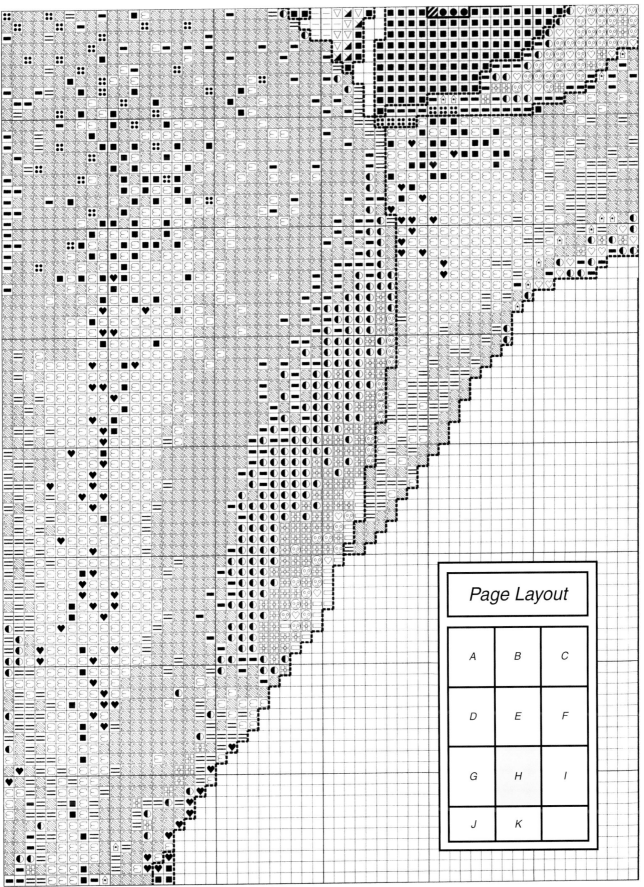

Red Tulips
Chart H

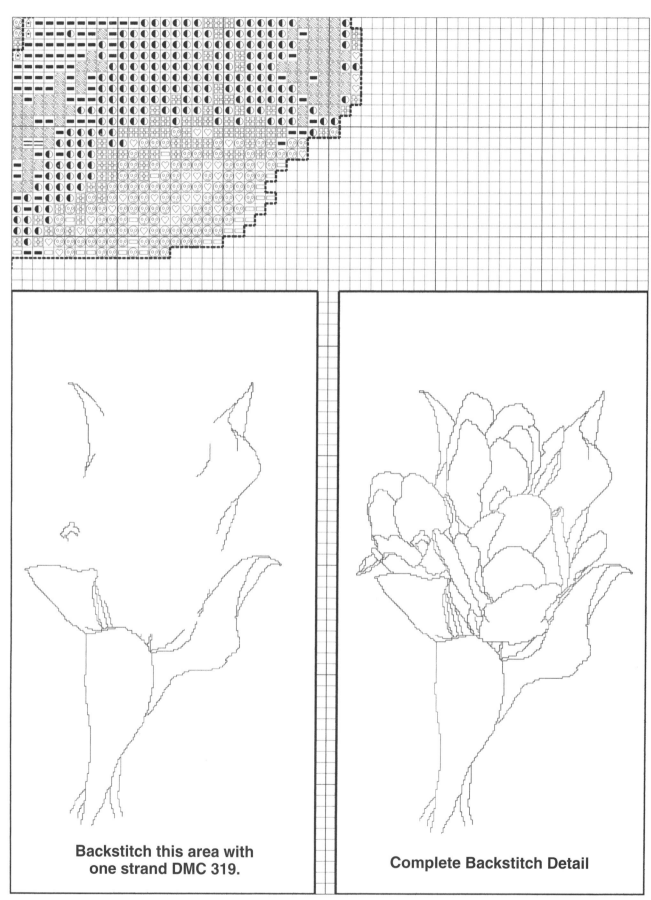

Backstitch this area with one strand DMC 319.

Complete Backstitch Detail

Red Tulips
Chart I

House of White Birches, Berne, Indiana 46711   AnniesAttic.com

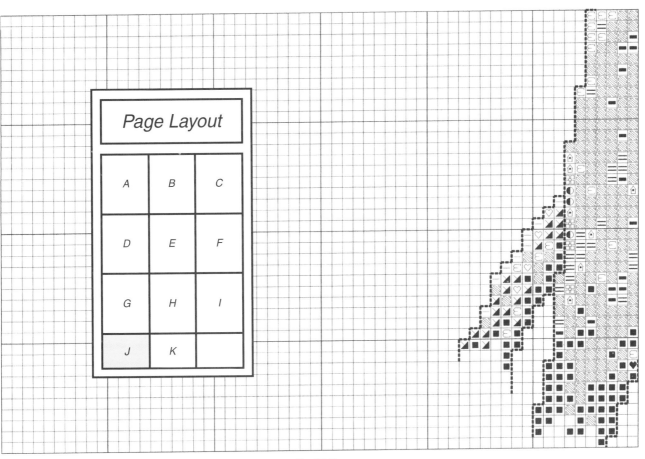

Red Tulips
Chart J

Red Tulips Color Key

ℤ	Anchor: 20	Ɛ	DMC: 367	◪	DMC: 902
✕	Anchor: 22	☺	DMC: 368	◣	DMC: 987
⊘	Anchor: 44	▭	DMC: 369	▨	DMC: 988
★	Anchor: 45	♥	DMC: 501	■	DMC: 3345
♡	Anchor: 214	⌂	DMC: 502	—	DMC: 3348
◖	Anchor: 215	⊞	DMC: 503	▽	DMC: 3364
▬	Anchor: 216	•	DMC: 522	●	DMC: 3371
◥	Anchor: 259	◑	DMC: 666	☆	DMC: 3801
∩	DMC: 304	♥	DMC: 814	∷	DMC: 3815
═	DMC: 320	T	DMC: 815	◉	Anchor: 9046
ⲭ	DMC: 321				

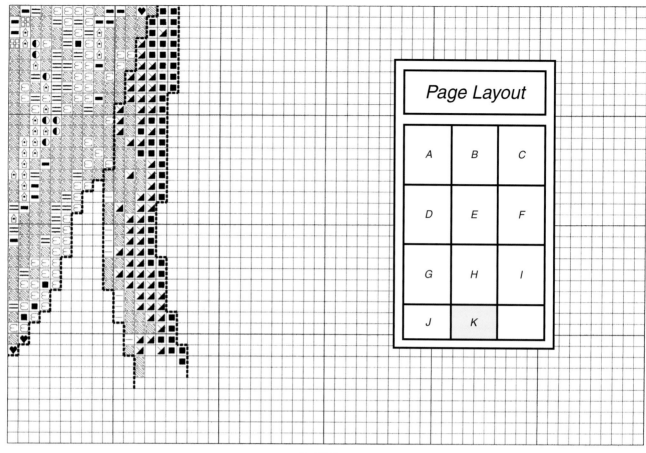

Red Tulips
Chart K

Red Tulips Color Key

Ƶ Anchor: 20	Ɛ DMC: 367	⚏ DMC: 902
✕ Anchor: 22	☺ DMC: 368	◢ DMC: 987
⊘ Anchor: 44	▭ DMC: 369	▨ DMC: 988
★ Anchor: 45	♥ DMC: 501	■ DMC: 3345
♡ Anchor: 214	⌂ DMC: 502	— DMC: 3348
◑ Anchor: 215	▦ DMC: 503	▽ DMC: 3364
▬ Anchor: 216	• DMC: 522	● DMC: 3371
◗ Anchor: 259	◍ DMC: 666	☆ DMC: 3801
∩ DMC: 304	♥ DMC: 814	∷ DMC: 3815
= DMC: 320	⊤ DMC: 815	⬡ Anchor: 9046
⊥ DMC: 321		

How to Stitch

Working From Charted Designs

A square on a chart corresponds to a space for a Cross-Stitch on the stitching surface. The symbol in a square shows the floss color to be used for the stitch. The width and height for the design stitch-area are given. The middle of each design is marked with a white circle.

Fabrics

Our front cover model was worked on Queen Anne's Lace 28-count Jobelan by Wichelt. Jobelan is an even-weave fabric that has the same number of horizontal and vertical threads (or blocks of threads) per inch. That number is called the thread count.

The size of the design is determined by the size of the even-weave fabric on which you work. Use the chart below as a guide to determine the finished size of a design on various popular sizes of cross-stitch fabric.

Designer Marc Saastad also suggests stitching with Queen Anne's Lace 32-count Jobelan by Wichelt.

Thread Count	Number of Stitches in Design				
	10	20	30	40	50
14-count	¾"	1⅜"	2⅛"	2⅞"	3⅝"
16-count	⅝"	1¼"	1⅞"	2½"	3⅛"
18-count	½"	1⅛"	1⅝"	2¼"	2¾"
25-count	⅜"	⅞"	1¼"	1⅝"	2"
28-count	⅜"	¾"	1"	1⅜"	1¾"
32-count	¼"	⅝"	⅞"	1¼"	1½"

(measurements are given to the nearest ⅛")

Needles

A blunt-tipped tapestry needle, size 24 or 26, is used for stitching on most 14-count to 28-count fabrics. The higher the needle number, the smaller the needle. The correct-size needle is easy to thread with the amount of floss required, but is not so large that it will distort the holes in the fabric. The following chart indicates the appropriate-size needle for each size of fabric, along with the suggested number of strands of floss to use.

Fabric	Strands of Floss	Tapestry Needle Size
14-count	2	24 or 26
16-count	2	24, 26 or 28
18-count	1 or 2	26 or 28
25-count	1	26 or 28
28-count	1	26 or 28
32-count over two threads	2	28

Floss

Our front cover model was stitched using 1 strand for cross-stitch and backstitches with DMC and Anchor 6-strand embroidery floss. Floss color numbers are given. Each design in this book uses both DMC and Anchor floss. Designer Marc Saastad has chosen each color and does not recommend changing the manufacturer given. Cut floss into comfortable working lengths; we suggest about 18 inches.

Getting Started

To begin in an unstitched area, bring threaded needle from back to front of fabric. Hold an inch of the end against the back, and then hold it in place with your first few stitches. To end threads and begin new ones next to existing stitches, weave through the backs of several stitches.

The Stitches

The number of strands used for Cross-Stitches will be determined by the thread count of the fabric used. Refer to the Needles chart to determine the number of strands used for Cross-Stitches. Use one strand for Backstitches.

Cross-Stitch

The Cross-Stitch is formed in two motions. Follow the numbering in Fig. 1 and bring needle up at 1, down at 2, up at 3, down at 4, to complete the stitch. Work horizontal rows of stitches (Fig. 2) wherever possible. Bring thread up at 1, work half of each stitch across the row, and then complete the stitches on your return.

Fig. 1
Cross-Stitch

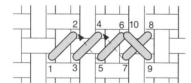

Fig. 2
Cross-Stitch
Horizontal Row

Backstitch

Backstitches are worked after Cross-Stitches have been completed. They may slope in any direction and are occasionally worked over more than one square of fabric. Fig. 3 shows the progression of several stitches; bring thread up at odd numbers and down at even numbers. Frequently you must choose where to end one Backstitch color and begin the next color. Choose the object that should appear closest to you. Backstitch around that shape with the appropriate color, and then Backstitch the areas behind it with adjacent color(s).

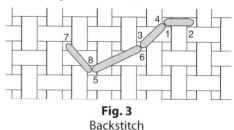

Fig. 3
Backstitch

For your convenience, we have included drawings that feature Backstitch placement. Backstitches for the leaves and stems are shown with straight lines. Backstitches for the flowers are shown with dotted lines.

Planning a Project

Before you stitch, decide how large to cut fabric. Determine the stitched size, and then allow enough additional fabric around the design plus 4 inches more on each side for use in finishing and mounting.

Cut your fabric exactly true, right along the holes of the fabric. Some raveling may occur as you handle the fabric. To minimize raveling along the raw edges, use an overcast basting stitch, machine zigzag stitch, or masking tape, which you can cut away when you are finished.

Finishing Needlework

When you have finished stitching, dampen your embroidery (or, if soiled, wash in lukewarm mild soapsuds and rinse well). Roll in a towel to remove excess moisture. Place facedown on a dry towel or padded surface, and press carefully until dry and smooth. Make sure all thread ends are well anchored and clipped closely. Proceed with desired finishing. ■

E-mail: Customer_Service@whitebirches.com

HOUSE of
WHITE
BIRCHES
PUBLISHERS
SINCE 1947

Splendid Florals is published by DRG, 306 East Parr Road, Berne, IN 46711. Printed in USA. Copyright © 2010 DRG. All rights reserved. This publication may not be reproduced in part or in whole without written permission from the publisher.

RETAIL STORES: If you would like to carry this pattern book or any other DRG publications, visit DRGwholesale.com

Every effort has been made to ensure that the instructions in this publication are complete and accurate. We cannot, however, take responsibility for human error, typographical mistakes or variations in individual work. Please visit AnniesCustomerCare.com to check for pattern updates.

STAFF

Editor: Barb Sprunger
Technical Editor: Marla Laux
Copy Supervisor: Michelle Beck
Copy Editor: Amanda Scheerer
Production Artist Supervisor:
  Erin Augsburger
Graphic Artists: Glenda Chamberlain,
  Edith Teegarden

Art Director: Brad Snow
Assistant Art Director: Nick Pierce
Photography Supervisor:
  Tammy Christian
Photography: Matthew Owen
Photo Stylist: Tammy Steiner

ISBN: 978-1-59012-229-7

2 3 4 5 6 7 8 9